Adelma Grenier Simmons

World of Fragrance

Potpourri and Sachets from Caprilands

Photographed by George Gregory Wieser

MALLARD PRESS

An Imprint of BDD Promotional Book Company, Inc.
666 Fifth Avenue
New York, NY 10103

This book is meant to be educational in nature and is in no way meant to be used for self-treatment or self-diagnosis. Keep in mind that excess quantities of some herbs can be dangerous. The editors have attempted to include, wherever appropriate, cautions and guidelines for using the herbs and herbal recipes in the book. Yet, we realize that it is impossible for us to anticipate every conceivable use of herbs and every possible problem any use could cause. Moreover, we cannot know just what kinds of physical reactions or allergies some of you might have to substances discussed in this book.

For this reason, Mallard Press cannot assume responsibility for the effects of using the herbs or other information in this book. And we urge that all potentially serious health problems be managed by a physician.

Copyright © 1992 by Adelma Grenier Simmons
Photographs copyright © 1992 by
George Gregory Wieser

Produced by Wieser & Wieser, Inc.
118 East 25th Street,
New York, NY 10010

Editorial Development by Beverly Pennacchini
Design, Typography and Production by Tony Meisel
Photographic Styling by Laurie Pepin

Mallard Press and its accompanying design and logo are trademarks of the BDD Promotional Book Company, Inc.
First published in the United States of America
in 1992 by The Mallard Press.

ISBN 0-7924-5618-1

Contents

Capturing the
World of Fragrance

The fragrant things of the world have a special romantic appeal. To walk in a garden of aromatic herbs is a rewarding experience. For the fragrance herb gardener, there is the additional reward of collecting summer's bounty and bringing the garden inside for winter enjoyment in the form of fragrant potpourri.

Historically, potpourri was not just pleasant but necessary. Improper sanitation, and the fear of fresh air, made the smell of flowers and spices a welcome relief to mask the accumulated odors of the rushes covering the stone or earthen floors.

It was the duty of a proper housewife to make potpourri, sweet bags and pomanders. The rose jar was kept on the table in the best room, and, after the cleaning was done, it was opened and stirred to scent the room and freshen the air. Sweet bags, filled with lavender, lemon verbena, with herbs and spice mixtures, were fitted to the backs of chairs and placed in closets and linen presses. Sweet herbs were strewn on the floors of church and home.

Many recipes for fragrances have been concocted. Some of these recipes found their way into stillroom books and were treasured as family heirlooms. Others were included in popular herbals and have become our common inheritance.

In this, our Caprilands Stillroom Book, we have presented brief histories of the essential materials that compose potpourri, as well as directions for growing and preserving them. To this we have added a few old recipes for scented things, and some of our own which we think are especially pleasing. It is such a sad waste of the fragrant flowers and herbs of the garden to allow them to drop to the ground unheeded, when, with a little care you can enjoy their fragrance throughout the winter.

Midsummer Mints

There are few plants in the garden as loved and useful, or as despised as the mints. To know them is to love them-and to be wary of their bold entrances into every domain of the garden. Still it would be hard to face a springtime garden without the curls of mint pushing though the brown soil like hundreds of small green roses opening up to the new season.

As we walk through the garden we can smell the cool odor of mint everywhere. It is indisputably a plant for tasting and smelling in hot summer weather. In ancient Greece and Rome, mint was a scent used by rich and poor. It was the custom to rub tables with it before guests were seated. To scent a room, hang bunches of mint from open doors or archways where a breeze will release the aroma, or tie them to screen doors to send cool odors through the house. When you are entertaining, place a sprig of mint on each napkin at the table.

Mints make fine terrace or patio plants. They thrive in redwood tubs, in large clay or pottery containers, or in plant pockets in terrace pavements. In using mints this way, be sure to provide drainage and evenly moist soil. Clip them back occasionally.

Orange Mint

The Orange Mint is one of the most fragrant plants in the garden and certainly the sweetest of the Mints. The clean citrus scent combines with Lavender and Bergamot, which it resembles in color. It dries well, keeping a good green color.

Peppermint

Peppermint is too strong for the sweet jars, but is wonderful in a more medicinal type mixture that can be used as one uses menthol. Its prime value is to clear the head and use as the ancient scholars used the mints, to clear the brain.

Mint Geranium

The large velvety leaves of the Mint Geranium combine well with the true Mints in the making of a clean smelling somewhat medicinal (but pleasantly so) potpourri. The leaves retain their heart shape well when pressed and dried and are quite decorative.

Mint Jar

A Potpourri to Clear the Head and Speed Up Mental Processes

2 cups dried lavender
1 cup dried mint (mix equal parts orange mint, spearmint, mint geranium leaves)
1/2 cup dried culinary thyme
1/4 cup rosemary
few drops of essential oils of lavender, thyme and bergamot
dried red geranium petals, blue bachelor's-button and delphinium

Combine ingredients and store in apothecary jars. When you're entertaining, turn some of this mixture out into a pewter or silver bowl. Stir slightly to release the fresh scent. An excellent potpourri for a desk or worktable, perhaps in an antique sugar bowl.

Lemon Zest

Lemon varieties are among the most fragrant of garden herbs. There is no other odor that can match the lemons for freshness. The scent is reminiscent of such pleasant things as a Victorian house with high cool rooms, closed shutters keeping out the heat of the day, or a sunny day in a Guatemala, where one can fill one's pockets with the leaves of the native Lemon Verbena bush.

Lemon Verbena, came from the Southwest via the spanish conquest and eventually arrived in England in approximately 1784 where it was immediately accepted for the fresh, cool odor it imparted to fragrant preparations. Other lemon varieties, however, such as balm and thyme, appear in old still books as having "an admirable virtue to alter melancholy." They were most often steeped as teas to cure feverish colds and improve attitudes.

The Lemons make delightful patio plants. Place lemon plants in a tub where they can be brushed as people walk by to release their clean odor. Plant lemon thyme in the cracks of walk ways or patio stones so that its fresh scent is released as people walk. Often, lemon leaves were used fresh as a garnish for sponge cakes or set on a sill over a sink to treat the cook to a breath of the past, an odor from a far away place.

As the lemons come from a variety of species, growing instructions vary widely, according to the family to which it belongs. Lemon Balm is a hardy perennial which may be grown from seed, planted in either spring or fall, and self sows in some situations. It winters well. The lemon geranium can be planted outside as soon as the danger of frost has past. Scented geraniums must be wintered indoors. Lemon Verbena is a tender perennial tree. There is no readily available or viable seed, therefore most plants are grown from cuttings, and must winter indoors.

Lemon Verbena

There is no odor quite like that of the Lemon Verbena, which is known as Vervain, the herb of enchantment, in the south of France. The leaves are very fragrant, although their scent is somewhat transient. It is best when combined with Lemon Balm and Lemon Peel. Lemon Oil may also be added to renew faded odors. Leaves with a little scent will still taste good as a tea. It can grow as a topiary tree by training on a support stake and cutting the lower shoots so that one stem emerges to branch out at the top, making a fragrant umbrella of leaves.

Lemon Balm

Lemon Balm has a delightful odor, attractive to the bees, resembling Lemon Verbena with the added advantage that it will live over the winter. It grows into a small bush and the height increases in the second year to 2 feet or more. Its wrinkled leaf is very decorative in the early spring when it emerges from the ground, and can thrive in sun or shade. Lemon Balm is reputed to be a "Balm for troubled spirits," but also makes an excellent tea and the fragrant leaves retain their refreshing odor well when dried and therefore are a good addition to potpourri.

Prince Rupert Crispum

The Lemon Geranium is second only to the old fashioned Rose in the memories of those who attempt to reconstruct a garden of the past. Like the rose there are many varieties with this refreshing lemon scent, however the prince Rupert is the sturdiest, and the most lemon. During the space of one summer in the garden under even fair conditions this will become a small shrub. Put in decorative terra cotta pots and allow it to grow as large as it wishes. It can be a pleasant addition to a terrace landscape or a flower pot garden. Prince Rupert also makes a delightful addition to hanging basket arrangements, or window box plantings. While the scent is strongly lemon, it blends with other odors pleasantly.

Lemon Verbena Jar

It causeth the mind and heart to become merry

1 cup dried lemon verbena leaves
1 cup dried lemon balm leaves
rind of 1 lemon, dried and grated
1/2 cup each dried petals from forsythia, calendula,
    lemon geranium, lemon-scented marigold, lemon
    thyme
1 ounce orris root with 6 drops of lemon verbena oil

Combine all ingredients, then turn into small apothecary jars. Press some of the yellow flowers against the sides of the jar for color. Tie the top with yellow and green velvet ribbon.

The Lyrical Lavenders

Lavender is one of the most ancient fragrances. It came to England with the Romans and found its happiest home there. It was used by the Greeks and Romans much as we use it today: for its clean sweet scent in washing water, soaps, pomades and perfuming sheets. It was a strewing herb in medieval times and a medicine believed to cure 43 ills of the flesh and spirit. Lavender has always been used to attract the bees and it produces an epicure's honey. It was also reputed to be a preserver of virtue, and was often used in wedding wreaths and bridal crowns, as a symbol of the brides innocence and purity.

The entire Lavender family is highly scented. Both the leaves and blossoms are used, although the blooms give off the most odor and carry the characteristic color. Lavender used in varying amounts will improve almost all potpourri and is also useful for the color that it adds to a glass jar. Its clean odor may be the necessary cool element needed to clam an overpowering mixture.

Trying picking bouquets of the blossoms and placing them in vases and baskets in the house. They are not only decorative, but impart a lovely scent, and if the weather is not unseasonably moist, the flower heads will dry perfectly for later use. Cut the blossoms when they are fully out, or the color will fade. Lavender is also stuffed into divan or sofa cushions to keep furniture clean smelling, or tied in sprigs behind curtains to freshen the air. Small lavender pillows can be placed in the corners of drawers to sweeten linens.

It is best to start your Lavender beds from plants, although seed sown in the late fall or very early spring will usually produce some seedlings. Lavenders are hardy perennials. The varieties Vera and Spica are hardy as far North as Nova Scotia. Sun, lime and drainage are the three requirements for successful growing. In winter a cover of boughs of evergreen or salt hay is desirable.

Hidcote

A hardy variety of lavender with branched narrow leaves and a dark blue flower. This makes a fine ornamental border plant, and may even grow large enough to be used as an unclipped hedge. Hidcote is a lovely addition to a bee and butterfly garden, or a fragrance garden and dries well for use in many fragrant mixtures. Lavender blossoms were often used as a tisane to cure nervous headaches.

Jean Davis

A hardy variety of lavender with pinkish white blossoms. When combined with Hidcote, this contrast of colors makes a beautiful and fragrant border for any garden, and is also useful in dried and fresh lavender table arrangements. Jean Davis, like all lavenders is fragrant and delightful in potpourri, or braided into a permanently sweet smelling wreath.

Vera and Spica

The hardiest and most common of the lavenders, these are perennials even in New England and well worth growing. Their blossoms are blue and leaves a silvery gray. Sprays of lavender were used by the harvesters in England-worn under their hats they were thought to stop sunstroke and headaches caused by the sum.

Moist Potpourri

Lavender for lovers true

1 cup dried lavender
3 cups dried rose petals
1 teaspoon each of allspice, cinnamon and coriander
1 tablespoon each of cloves, grated nutmeg, and anise
1/4 cup each of patchouli leaves and powdered orris root
1/4 ounce each of oil of rose and oil of rose geranium
3 cups of a mixture made of dried rosemary, lemon balm, and lemon verbena leaves.

In a covered crock, mix rose petals with the bay salt and leave for one week, turning daily. Add spices and let stand for another week, turning daily. At the end of the two weeks add the lavender, patchouli, orris root, and oils. Let stand for a few weeks, then mix in leaves of dried rosemary, lemon balm, and lemon verbena. Stir frequently with a wooden spoon or cinnamon stick.

27

The Romance of the Rose

The rose, special flower of midsummer, has always been symbolic, generally, of love and romance, although in one of the later books on the Language of Flowers, there are forty entries for the meaning of the Rose ranging from love to shame, from youth to age, from war to tranquility. The rose became a symbol of war in the fifteenth century when it was adopted as the badge of the rival English Houses of York and Lancaster. Brides, and indeed both sexes in ancient times, were crowned with a chaplet of red and white roses, and instead of rice, were pelted with petals as part of the celebration.

Roses are highly prized for their value in fragrant mixtures. Rose petals are used in a wide variety of potpourri, both for their everlasting color and subtle scent. Attar of roses or rose oil, made from steeping roses in oil is indispensable in the creation of potpourri. Often only one drop is necessary to impart a fragrant and lasting odor to any blend. Rose water is used as an invigorating after bath splash, and in the preparation of many delicious dishes.

Roses can be propagated from seeds, cuttings, or buddings, but it's easiest to buy nursery stock. Roses will grow well in a good, well-drained garden soil. Blossoms that you intend to dry should be picked on a day when the air is dry. For perfect rose petals, pick before they are completely blown. Remove the petals and place them on a large sheet of blotting paper and cover with a heavy piece of glass. Leave until dry.

Rosa Damascena

The damask rose is associated with the famous "Valley of the Roses" in Bulgaria where hundreds of individual rose farmers cultivate this fragrant rose. Many of these distilled their own essences in old fashioned, primitive stills. It is said that it takes 10,000 pounds of damask roses to make one pound of oil.

Apothecary's Rose

One of the oldest varieties of roses referred to as a "June" rose, and known for its sweet and powerful fragrance. The apothecary's rose, like other old June varieties, such as the Damask, are so fragrant that they are used in the production of rose oil, and also can be combined as petals in potpourri that requires no essence. Although this is an heirloom variety, it is especially hardy.

Rober's Lemon Rose

This is a scented geranium, and not a rose proper, but this plant's long thick leaves have the sweetest of rose scents. Rober's lemon rose looks rather like a tomato plant as it starts growth. This plant is very hardy, and will yield hundreds of the sweetest leaves in the garden which may be used in potpourri or tea.

Rose Jar

To bathe young buds in dews from heaven

1 quart dried rose petals
1 cup each of dried lavender flowers and rose
    geranium leaves
1/2 cup patchouli
1/4 cup sandalwood chips and vetiver, mixed
1 teaspoon each of powdered benzoin, cinnamon
    and cloves
2 teaspoons frankincense and myrrh, mixed
2 tonka beans, ground
1/4 cup allspice
10 drops rose oil
1 cup orris root

Mix first eight ingredients thoroughly, then add the rose oil and orris root. Mix again and stir well. If this amount of orris seems excessive remember that this is a base mixture to which you can add flowers of the season right up to fall. After it is finished, close the jar for at least two weeks (a month is better), then it will be ready to enjoy.

TO

THE QVEE

MOST EXCE

MAIESTI

The Sweet Sandalwoods

The odor of sandalwood is one of great fascination. It is reminiscent of the opening of a chest filled with oriental silks, or of an elaborately carved fan whipping the air in the hot moist atmosphere of an Indian jungle. It also recalls the Victorian parlors of New England. I shall never smell sandalwood without a momentary glimpse of this fascinating sanctuary of my youth.

This "sanders wood" of the old recipe books does not have a charm for all people. In fact, there are many who at first are unable to sense its faded, faintly spicy odor, though, if it is burned where it can penetrate and linger in the rooms, there are few who do not enjoy it. Sandalwood must be heated to make it the most odorous. Sandalwood chips are best for the purpose of maing potpourri, and they add that indefinable something to a jar. Blocks can be placed in drawers to keep clothes smelling fresh. The odor of sandalwood discourages moths.

White Sandalwood

White sandalwood is a small tree, 20 to 30 feet high and native to the Malabar coast. It is also found in New Caledonia. Though it has a growth potential of 30 feet, it seldom attains its full height, but remains a bush or a low growing tree. From early times, its wood was highly valued for its sweet odor. It was employed in the making of musical instruments, particularly those that were used in sacred ceremonies. It was also used for burning at the sacrifices of idols and was later a part of the incense used in the Jewish synagogues. For more domestic purposes, fans were made of it, and it was used to line boxes, to make chests secure against the inroads of moths.

Red Sandalwood

A large tree indigenous to Ceylon and India. The wood of this variety is very heavy and extremely hard, suitable for the making of long lasting carved furniture. It is still in use today in the production of such musical instruments as lyres and lutes.

Simmering Sandalwood

1 cup sandalwood chips or shavings
1/2 cup lavender flowers
1/2 cup rose petals
2 teaspoons frankincense and myrrh, mixed
1 teaspoon vetiver
1 teaspoon cinnamon
1 teaspoon allspice

Combine all ingredients and place in an apothecary jar. To simmer, place potpourri in a small pot with water and allow to simmer over a tea candle, or, place in a bowl with water and set it atop a radiator to steam scent the room in the winter.

Fixatives to Hold Flower Fragrances

Fixatives from the animal or plant world are used to hold the fragrance of potpourri ingredients. Animal fixatives include ambergris, civet, and musk. The odor of fixatives alone, in particular, ambergris from the sperm whale, is disagreeable, but when combined with fragrant things, it absorbs and enhances the essences.

The plant fixatives I use most are orris root, and tonka bean. Orris root comes from Iris florentina, a variety of I. germanica. The fresh root is dug, peeled and sun-dried, then stored for two years to develop the scent. It is then ground and emits the violet odor for which it is known. Orris root is the most common fixative for potpourri as it is easily obtainable.

Essential Oils

When essences or essential oils are included in recipes, the distilled plant oil is indicated. These are generally volatile oils that evaporate at room temperatures. They occur in secretory cells, reservoirs, glands of flowers, barks, fruits, and leaves. Most oils are obtained by steam distillation. A very common oil is Attar of roses or rose "otto" as it is sometimes called. Other oils used in the making of potpourri include oil of violet, carnation, jasmine, lemon verbena, and orange blossom.

Spices for Potpourri

Allspice: A member of the myrtle family native to the West Indies. Allspice adds a wonderful touch of bayrum to potpourri.

Calamus root

This product of Acorus calamus comes from France and Belgium. Calamus root, and the oil derived from it add a mellow and spicy odor to potpourri.

Cinnamon bark or sticks

A member of the laurel family which yields a spicy element which was once the chief ingredient in the manufacture of the holy oils of the bible.

Cloves

A member of the myrtle family native to Zanzibar, British Malaya, Ceylon, Indian, Madagascar, and Penang. The citrus scent adds a lovely orange touch to potpourri.

Frankincense

Native to the East, frankincense gives us the most used and treasured of all the sweet odors. The odor of frankincense is not discernible in potpourri, unless the mixture is warm or moist. However, it is a fixative and adds stability to a mixture.

Myrrh

Native to Arabia, the fragrant bark and gum is not only sweet smelling, but in the past was used to soothe a sore throat, and as a purifying agent.

Patchouli

Native to the tropics, these large, musk-smelling leaves give depth to potpourri and have fixative powers as well.

Tonka Bean

Native to Brazil and Ceylon, Venezuela, British Guiana and Africa, this bean provides one of the most concentrated of floral odors. It is overpowering in its sweetness, heavy with the smell of coumarin. The ground beans are important for good potpourri, since they act as a fixative and an intensifier, sharpening other odors while losing their own.

Vetiver root

Comes mainly from Java although small amounts do grow in Louisiana and the West Indies. It has a fragrant root with the odor of violets or sandalwood. As a fixative in potpourri, it never seems to lose its fragrance.

When to Make Potpourri

Through the summer and far into autumn, the good herb gardener is busy harvesting. Airtight tin containers hold chip-dry rose petals, aromatic lavender, lemon verbena, orange mint, and other members of the mint family. Large boxes or drawers in an old dresser hold a colorful selection of dried flowers, not necessarily fragrant, for decoration within the glass jars of potpourri.

It is important to keep drying material in a dry, well ventilated location, where air is able to circulate. Moisture must be avoided. Leafy materials can be tied in loose bunches and hung in a well ventilated place until dry. Petals can be placed on a sheet of blotting paper and covered with glass until dry.

The sun will fade the colors of the brightest, freshest lavender or roses, so keep potpourri jars and drying materials out of the sun or strong light, except on occasion.

How to care for Potpourri

Potpourri can be renewed several ways. A few drops of alcohol or brandy will revive a fading, fainting odor. Add a few patchouli leaves, some fresh lavender or drops of essential oils and extra spice will help also.

Removing the whole from the jar and remixing is the best way to restore it. Some new petals may be added with drops of oil. If you wish to make a new jar and discard the old, store the faded mixture in a tight container and burn it as incense. Although it may no longer have a strong odor when dry, if burned, it will smell as sweet as the Indies.

A mixture that will last in a jar for years will fade in a few months if put in a cloth or silk container. keep the bulk of your potpourri in a covered jar and use only a little at a time in bags.

Sachets and Scented Pillows

Sachets are made simply by tying up a fragrant dried mixture of potpourri in a square of organdy or fine net. Decorate with little dried roses or everlastings and a bow. Antique glass containers with a sachet in them make delightful gifts.

Covers for scented pillows are made of organdy, fine net, or silk, but put the more sturdy fragrances of pine and patchouli into soft felt or homespun. Pieces of brocade, velvet, and chintz also make useful covers. For these small pillows, make an attractive case of one of these materials and a slightly smaller lining of muslin to hold the fragrant mixture.

Use prolific plants from the herb garden for the bulk of fragrant material for pillows. Lemon balm is one of the most leafy herbs; lemon and camphor southernwoods also produce an abundance of foliage with a clean, penetrating and lasting scent. Combine any of these with cuttings of rosemary, bergamot, thyme and bay leaves, and a generous amount of dried orange and lemon peel.